A Note to Parents & Teachers—

Welcome to I See Insects from Xist Publishing! These books are designed to inspire discovery and delight in the youngest readers. Each book features very simple sentences with visual cues to help beginners read their very first text.

You can help each child develop a lifetime love of reading right from the very start. Here are some ways to help a beginning reader get going:

 Read the book aloud as a first introduction

 Run your fingers below the words as you read each line

 Give the child the chance to finish the sentences or read repeating words while you read the rest.

 Encourage the child to read aloud every day!

Copyright © Xist Publishing 2022
First Edition
All Rights Reserved.
No portion of this book may be reproduced without express permission from the publisher.

Published proudly in the State of Texas, USA by Xist Publishing
www.xistpublishing.com
24200 Southwest Freeway Suite 402- 290 Rosenberg, TX 77471
All images licensed from Adobe Stock
First Edition

Hardcover ISBN: 978-1-5324-3350-4
Perfect Bound ISBN: 978-1-5324-4144-8
Saddle Stitch ISBN: 978-1-5324-2867-8
eISBN: 978-1-5324-2842-5

I See Insects
Lice

written by **August Hoeft**

INSPIRING DISCOVERY & DELIGHT

I see lice.

The louse is tan.

The louse is very small.

8

The louse eats blood.

10

The louse lives in hair.

I see lice.

Things to do next!

Write a Sentence

I see a_____.

Drawing

Make a drawing of your favorite insect.

Sharing

Talk to your classmates about your favorite picture in this book. Explain to them why you like it.

WORD LIST

blood
eats
hair
I
in
is
lice
lives

louse
see
small
tan
the
very

www.ingramcontent.com/pod-product-compliance
Lightning Source LLC
LaVergne TN
LVHW070015090426
835508LV00048B/3422